Religious Poems

John Greenleaf Whittier

Contents

RELIGIOUS POEMS

BY

John Greenleaf Whittier

THE ANSWER.

Spare me, dread angel of reproof,
And let the sunshine weave to-day
Its gold-threads in the warp and woof
Of life so poor and gray.

Spare me awhile; the flesh is weak.
These lingering feet, that fain would stray
Among the flowers, shall some day seek
The strait and narrow way.

Take off thy ever-watchful eye,
The awe of thy rebuking frown;
The dullest slave at times must sigh
To fling his burdens down;

To drop his galley's straining oar,
And press, in summer warmth and calm,
The lap of some enchanted shore
Of blossom and of balm.

Grudge not my life its hour of bloom,
My heart its taste of long desire;
This day be mine: be those to come
As duty shall require.

The deep voice answered to my own,
Smiting my selfish prayers away;
"To-morrow is with God alone,
And man hath but to-day.

"Say not, thy fond, vain heart within,
The Father's arm shall still be wide,
When from these pleasant ways of sin
Thou turn'st at eventide.

"'Cast thyself down,' the tempter saith,
'And angels shall thy feet upbear.'
He bids thee make a lie of faith,
And blasphemy of prayer.

"Though God be good and free be heaven,
No force divine can love compel;
And, though the song of sins forgiven
May sound through lowest hell,

"The sweet persuasion of His voice
Respects thy sanctity of will.
He giveth day: thou hast thy choice
To walk in darkness still;

"As one who, turning from the light,
Watches his own gray shadow fall,
Doubting, upon his path of night,
If there be day at all!

"No word of doom may shut thee out,
No wind of wrath may downward whirl,
No swords of fire keep watch about

The open gates of pearl;

"A tenderer light than moon or sun,
Than song of earth a sweeter hymn,
May shine and sound forever on,
And thou be deaf and dim.

"Forever round the Mercy-seat
The guiding lights of Love shall burn;
But what if, habit-bound, thy feet
Shall lack the will to turn?

"What if thine eye refuse to see,
Thine ear of Heaven's free welcome fail,
And thou a willing captive be,
Thyself thy own dark jail?

"Oh, doom beyond the saddest guess,
As the long years of God unroll,
To make thy dreary selfishness
The prison of a soul!

"To doubt the love that fain would break
The fetters from thy self-bound limb;
And dream that God can thee forsake
As thou forsakest Him!"
1863.

THE ETERNAL GOODNESS.

O friends! with whom my feet have trod
The quiet aisles of prayer,
Glad witness to your zeal for God
And love of man I bear.

I trace your lines of argument;
Your logic linked and strong
I weigh as one who dreads dissent,
And fears a doubt as wrong.

But still my human hands are weak
To hold your iron creeds
Against the words ye bid me speak
My heart within me pleads.

Who fathoms the Eternal Thought?
Who talks of scheme and plan?
The Lord is God! He needeth not
The poor device of man.

I walk with bare, hushed feet the ground
Ye tread with boldness shod;
I dare not fix with mete and bound
The love and power of God.

Ye praise His justice; even such
His pitying love I deem
Ye seek a king; I fain would touch
The robe that hath no seam.

Ye see the curse which overbroods
A world of pain and loss;
I hear our Lord's beatitudes
And prayer upon the cross.

More than your schoolmen teach, within
Myself, alas! I know
Too dark ye cannot paint the sin,
Too small the merit show.

I bow my forehead to the dust,
I veil mine eyes for shame,
And urge, in trembling self-distrust,
A prayer without a claim.

I see the wrong that round me lies,
I feel the guilt within;
I hear, with groan and travail-cries,
The world confess its sin.

Yet, in the maddening maze of things,
And tossed by storm and flood,
To one fixed trust my spirit clings;
I know that God is good!

Not mine to look where cherubim
And seraphs may not see,
But nothing can be good in Him

Which evil is in me.

The wrong that pains my soul below
I dare not throne above,
I know not of His hate,--I know
His goodness and His love.

I dimly guess from blessings known
Of greater out of sight,
And, with the chastened Psalmist, own
His judgments too are right.

I long for household voices gone,
For vanished smiles I long,
But God hath led my dear ones on,
And He can do no wrong.

I know not what the future hath
Of marvel or surprise,
Assured alone that life and death
His mercy underlies.

And if my heart and flesh are weak
To bear an untried pain,
The bruised reed He will not break,
But strengthen and sustain.

No offering of my own I have,
Nor works my faith to prove;
I can but give the gifts He gave,
And plead His love for love.

And so beside the Silent Sea

I wait the muffled oar;
No harm from Him can come to me
On ocean or on shore.

I know not where His islands lift
Their fronded palms in air;
I only know I cannot drift
Beyond His love and care.

O brothers! if my faith is vain,
If hopes like these betray,
Pray for me that my feet may gain
The sure and safer way.

And Thou, O Lord! by whom are seen
Thy creatures as they be,
Forgive me if too close I lean
My human heart on Thee!
1865.

THE COMMON QUESTION.

Behind us at our evening meal
The gray bird ate his fill,
Swung downward by a single claw,
And wiped his hooked bill.

He shook his wings and crimson tail,
And set his head aslant,
And, in his sharp, impatient way,
Asked, "What does Charlie want?"

"Fie, silly bird!" I answered, "tuck
Your head beneath your wing,
And go to sleep;"--but o'er and o'er
He asked the self-same thing.

Then, smiling, to myself I said
How like are men and birds!
We all are saying what he says,
In action or in words.

The boy with whip and top and drum,
The girl with hoop and doll,
And men with lands and houses, ask
The question of Poor Poll.

However full, with something more
We fain the bag would cram;
We sigh above our crowded nets
For fish that never swam.

No bounty of indulgent Heaven
The vague desire can stay;
Self-love is still a Tartar mill
For grinding prayers alway.

The dear God hears and pities all;
He knoweth all our wants;
And what we blindly ask of Him
His love withholds or grants.

And so I sometimes think our prayers
Might well be merged in one;
And nest and perch and hearth and church
Repeat, "Thy will be done."

OUR MASTER.

Immortal Love, forever full,
Forever flowing free,
Forever shared, forever whole,
A never-ebbing sea!

Our outward lips confess the name
All other names above;
Love only knoweth whence it came
And comprehendeth love.

Blow, winds of God, awake and blow
The mists of earth away!
Shine out, O Light Divine, and show
How wide and far we stray!

Hush every lip, close every book,
The strife of tongues forbear;
Why forward reach, or backward look,
For love that clasps like air?

We may not climb the heavenly steeps
To bring the Lord Christ down
In vain we search the lowest deeps,
For Him no depths can drown.

Nor holy bread, nor blood of grape,
The lineaments restore
Of Him we know in outward shape
And in the flesh no more.

He cometh not a king to reign;
The world's long hope is dim;
The weary centuries watch in vain
The clouds of heaven for Him.

Death comes, life goes; the asking eye
And ear are answerless;
The grave is dumb, the hollow sky
Is sad with silentness.

The letter fails, and systems fall,
And every symbol wanes;
The Spirit over-brooding all
Eternal Love remains.

And not for signs in heaven above
Or earth below they look,
Who know with John His smile of love,
With Peter His rebuke.

In joy of inward peace, or sense
Of sorrow over sin,
He is His own best evidence,
His witness is within.

No fable old, nor mythic lore,
Nor dream of bards and seers,
No dead fact stranded on the shore

Of the oblivious years;--

But warm, sweet, tender, even yet
A present help is He;
And faith has still its Olivet,
And love its Galilee.

The healing of His seamless dress
Is by our beds of pain;
We touch Him in life's throng and press,
And we are whole again.

Through Him the first fond prayers are said
Our lips of childhood frame,
The last low whispers of our dead
Are burdened with His name.

Our Lord and Master of us all!
Whate'er our name or sign,
We own Thy sway, we hear Thy call,
We test our lives by Thine.

Thou judgest us; Thy purity
Doth all our lusts condemn;
The love that draws us nearer Thee
Is hot with wrath to them.

Our thoughts lie open to Thy sight;
And, naked to Thy glance,
Our secret sins are in the light
Of Thy pure countenance.

Thy healing pains, a keen distress

Thy tender light shines in;
Thy sweetness is the bitterness,
Thy grace the pang of sin.

Yet, weak and blinded though we be,
Thou dost our service own;
We bring our varying gifts to Thee,
And Thou rejectest none.

To Thee our full humanity,
Its joys and pains, belong;
The wrong of man to man on Thee
Inflicts a deeper wrong.

Who hates, hates Thee, who loves becomes
Therein to Thee allied;
All sweet accords of hearts and homes
In Thee are multiplied.

Deep strike Thy roots, O heavenly Vine,
Within our earthly sod,
Most human and yet most divine,
The flower of man and God!

O Love! O Life! Our faith and sight
Thy presence maketh one
As through transfigured clouds of white
We trace the noon-day sun.

So, to our mortal eyes subdued,
Flesh-veiled, but not concealed,
We know in Thee the fatherhood
And heart of God revealed.

We faintly hear, we dimly see,
In differing phrase we pray;
But, dim or clear, we own in Thee
The Light, the Truth, the Way!

The homage that we render Thee
Is still our Father's own;
No jealous claim or rivalry
Divides the Cross and Throne.

To do Thy will is more than praise,
As words are less than deeds,
And simple trust can find Thy ways
We miss with chart of creeds.

No pride of self Thy service hath,
No place for me and mine;
Our human strength is weakness, death
Our life, apart from Thine.

Apart from Thee all gain is loss,
All labor vainly done;
The solemn shadow of Thy Cross
Is better than the sun.

Alone, O Love ineffable!
Thy saving name is given;
To turn aside from Thee is hell,
To walk with Thee is heaven!

How vain, secure in all Thou art,
Our noisy championship
The sighing of the contrite heart

Is more than flattering lip.

Not Thine the bigot's partial plea,
Nor Thine the zealot's ban;
Thou well canst spare a love of Thee
Which ends in hate of man.

Our Friend, our Brother, and our Lord,
What may Thy service be?--
Nor name, nor form, nor ritual word,
But simply following Thee.

We bring no ghastly holocaust,
We pile no graven stone;
He serves thee best who loveth most
His brothers and Thy own.

Thy litanies, sweet offices
Of love and gratitude;
Thy sacramental liturgies,
The joy of doing good.

In vain shall waves of incense drift
The vaulted nave around,
In vain the minster turret lift
Its brazen weights of sound.

The heart must ring Thy Christmas bells,
Thy inward altars raise;
Its faith and hope Thy canticles,
And its obedience praise!
1866.

THE MEETING.

The two speakers in the meeting referred to in this poem were Avis Keene, whose very presence was a benediction, a woman lovely in spirit and person, whose words seemed a message of love and tender concern to her hearers; and Sibyl Jones, whose inspired eloquence and rare spirituality impressed all who knew her. In obedience to her apprehended duty she made visits of Christian love to various parts of Europe, and to the West Coast of Africa and Palestine.

The elder folks shook hands at last,
Down seat by seat the signal passed.
To simple ways like ours unused,
Half solemnized and half amused,
With long-drawn breath and shrug, my guest
His sense of glad relief expressed.
Outside, the hills lay warm in sun;
The cattle in the meadow-run
Stood half-leg deep; a single bird
The green repose above us stirred.
"What part or lot have you," he said,
"In these dull rites of drowsy-head?
Is silence worship? Seek it where
It soothes with dreams the summer air,
Not in this close and rude-benched hall,
But where soft lights and shadows fall,
And all the slow, sleep-walking hours

Glide soundless over grass and flowers!
From time and place and form apart,
Its holy ground the human heart,
Nor ritual-bound nor templeward
Walks the free spirit of the Lord!
Our common Master did not pen
His followers up from other men;
His service liberty indeed,
He built no church, He framed no creed;
But while the saintly Pharisee
Made broader his phylactery,
As from the synagogue was seen
The dusty-sandalled Nazarene
Through ripening cornfields lead the way
Upon the awful Sabbath day,
His sermons were the healthful talk
That shorter made the mountain-walk,
His wayside texts were flowers and birds,
Where mingled with His gracious words
The rustle of the tamarisk-tree
And ripple-wash of Galilee."

"Thy words are well, O friend," I said;
"Unmeasured and unlimited,
With noiseless slide of stone to stone,
The mystic Church of God has grown.
Invisible and silent stands
The temple never made with hands,
Unheard the voices still and small
Of its unseen confessional.
He needs no special place of prayer
Whose hearing ear is everywhere;
He brings not back the childish days

That ringed the earth with stones of praise,
Roofed Karnak's hall of gods, and laid
The plinths of Phil e's colonnade.
Still less He owns the selfish good
And sickly growth of solitude,--
The worthless grace that, out of sight,
Flowers in the desert anchorite;
Dissevered from the suffering whole,
Love hath no power to save a soul.
Not out of Self, the origin
And native air and soil of sin,
The living waters spring and flow,
The trees with leaves of healing grow.

"Dream not, O friend, because I seek
This quiet shelter twice a week,
I better deem its pine-laid floor
Than breezy hill or sea-sung shore;
But nature is not solitude
She crowds us with her thronging wood;
Her many hands reach out to us,
Her many tongues are garrulous;
Perpetual riddles of surprise
She offers to our ears and eyes;
She will not leave our senses still,
But drags them captive at her will
And, making earth too great for heaven,
She hides the Giver in the given.

"And so, I find it well to come
For deeper rest to this still room,
For here the habit of the soul
Feels less the outer world's control;

The strength of mutual purpose pleads
More earnestly our common needs;
And from the silence multiplied
By these still forms on either side,
The world that time and sense have known
Falls off and leaves us God alone.

"Yet rarely through the charmed repose
Unmixed the stream of motive flows,
A flavor of its many springs,
The tints of earth and sky it brings;
In the still waters needs must be
Some shade of human sympathy;
And here, in its accustomed place,
I look on memory's dearest face;
The blind by-sitter guesseth not
What shadow haunts that vacant spot;
No eyes save mine alone can see
The love wherewith it welcomes me!
And still, with those alone my kin,
In doubt and weakness, want and sin,
I bow my head, my heart I bare
As when that face was living there,
And strive (too oft, alas! in vain)
The peace of simple trust to gain,
Fold fancy's restless wings, and lay
The idols of my heart away.

"Welcome the silence all unbroken,
Nor less the words of fitness spoken,--
Such golden words as hers for whom
Our autumn flowers have just made room;
Whose hopeful utterance through and through

The freshness of the morning blew;
Who loved not less the earth that light
Fell on it from the heavens in sight,
But saw in all fair forms more fair
The Eternal beauty mirrored there.
Whose eighty years but added grace
And saintlier meaning to her face,--
The look of one who bore away
Glad tidings from the hills of day,
While all our hearts went forth to meet
The coming of her beautiful feet!
Or haply hers, whose pilgrim tread
Is in the paths where Jesus led;
Who dreams her childhood's Sabbath dream
By Jordan's willow-shaded stream,
And, of the hymns of hope and faith,
Sung by the monks of Nazareth,
Hears pious echoes, in the call
To prayer, from Moslem minarets fall,
Repeating where His works were wrought
The lesson that her Master taught,
Of whom an elder Sibyl gave,
The prophecies of Cuma 's cave.

"I ask no organ's soulless breath
To drone the themes of life and death,
No altar candle-lit by day,
No ornate wordsman's rhetoric-play,
No cool philosophy to teach
Its bland audacities of speech
To double-tasked idolaters
Themselves their gods and worshippers,
No pulpit hammered by the fist

Of loud-asserting dogmatist,
Who borrows for the Hand of love
The smoking thunderbolts of Jove.
I know how well the fathers taught,
What work the later schoolmen wrought;
I reverence old-time faith and men,
But God is near us now as then;
His force of love is still unspent,
His hate of sin as imminent;
And still the measure of our needs
Outgrows the cramping bounds of creeds;
The manna gathered yesterday
Already savors of decay;
Doubts to the world's child-heart unknown
Question us now from star and stone;
Too little or too much we know,
And sight is swift and faith is slow;
The power is lost to self-deceive
With shallow forms of make-believe.
W e walk at high noon, and the bells
Call to a thousand oracles,
But the sound deafens, and the light
Is stronger than our dazzled sight;
The letters of the sacred Book
Glimmer and swim beneath our look;
Still struggles in the Age's breast
With deepening agony of quest
The old entreaty: 'Art thou He,
Or look we for the Christ to be?'

"God should be most where man is least
So, where is neither church nor priest,
And never rag of form or creed

To clothe the nakedness of need,--
Where farmer-folk in silence meet,--
I turn my bell-unsummoned feet;'
I lay the critic's glass aside,
I tread upon my lettered pride,
And, lowest-seated, testify
To the oneness of humanity;
Confess the universal want,
And share whatever Heaven may grant.
He findeth not who seeks his own,
The soul is lost that's saved alone.
Not on one favored forehead fell
Of old the fire-tongued miracle,
But flamed o'er all the thronging host
The baptism of the Holy Ghost;
Heart answers heart: in one desire
The blending lines of prayer aspire;
'Where, in my name, meet two or three,'
Our Lord hath said, 'I there will be!'

"So sometimes comes to soul and sense
The feeling which is evidence
That very near about us lies
The realm of spiritual mysteries.
The sphere of the supernal powers
Impinges on this world of ours.
The low and dark horizon lifts,
To light the scenic terror shifts;
The breath of a diviner air
Blows down the answer of a prayer
That all our sorrow, pain, and doubt
A great compassion clasps about,
And law and goodness, love and force,

Are wedded fast beyond divorce.
Then duty leaves to love its task,
The beggar Self forgets to ask;
With smile of trust and folded hands,
The passive soul in waiting stands
To feel, as flowers the sun and dew,
The One true Life its own renew.

"So, to the calmly gathered thought
The innermost of truth is taught,
The mystery dimly understood,
That love of God is love of good,
And, chiefly, its divinest trace
In Him of Nazareth's holy face;
That to be saved is only this,--
Salvation from our selfishness,
From more than elemental fire,
The soul's unsanetified desire,
From sin itself, and not the pain
That warns us of its chafing chain;
That worship's deeper meaning lies
In mercy, and not sacrifice,
Not proud humilities of sense
And posturing of penitence,
But love's unforced obedience;
That Book and Church and Day are given
For man, not God,--for earth, not heaven,--
The blessed means to holiest ends,
Not masters, but benignant friends;
That the dear Christ dwells not afar,
The king of some remoter star,
Listening, at times, with flattered ear
To homage wrung from selfish fear,

But here, amidst the poor and blind,
The bound and suffering of our kind,
In works we do, in prayers we pray,
Life of our life, He lives to-day."
1868.

THE CLEAR VISION.

I did but dream. I never knew
What charms our sternest season wore.
Was never yet the sky so blue,
Was never earth so white before.
Till now I never saw the glow
Of sunset on yon hills of snow,
And never learned the bough's designs
Of beauty in its leafless lines.

Did ever such a morning break
As that my eastern windows see?
Did ever such a moonlight take
Weird photographs of shrub and tree?
Rang ever bells so wild and fleet
The music of the winter street?
Was ever yet a sound by half
So merry as yon school-boy's laugh?

O Earth! with gladness overfraught,
No added charm thy face hath found;
Within my heart the change is wrought,
My footsteps make enchanted ground.
From couch of pain and curtained room
Forth to thy light and air I come,

To find in all that meets my eyes
The freshness of a glad surprise.

Fair seem these winter days, and soon
Shall blow the warm west-winds of spring,
To set the unbound rills in tune
And hither urge the bluebird's wing.
The vales shall laugh in flowers, the woods
Grow misty green with leafing buds,
And violets and wind-flowers sway
Against the throbbing heart of May.

Break forth, my lips, in praise, and own
The wiser love severely kind;
Since, richer for its chastening grown,
I see, whereas I once was blind.
The world, O Father! hath not wronged
With loss the life by Thee prolonged;
But still, with every added year,
More beautiful Thy works appear!

As Thou hast made thy world without,
Make Thou more fair my world within;
Shine through its lingering clouds of doubt;
Rebuke its haunting shapes of sin;
Fill, brief or long, my granted span
Of life with love to thee and man;
Strike when thou wilt the hour of rest,
But let my last days be my best!
2d mo., 1868.

DIVINE COMPASSION.

Long since, a dream of heaven I had,
And still the vision haunts me oft;
I see the saints in white robes clad,
The martyrs with their palms aloft;
But hearing still, in middle song,
The ceaseless dissonance of wrong;
And shrinking, with hid faces, from the strain
Of sad, beseeching eyes, full of remorse and pain.

The glad song falters to a wail,
The harping sinks to low lament;
Before the still unlifted veil
I see the crowned foreheads bent,
Making more sweet the heavenly air,
With breathings of unselfish prayer;
And a Voice saith: "O Pity which is pain,
O Love that weeps, fill up my sufferings which remain!

"Shall souls redeemed by me refuse
To share my sorrow in their turn?
Or, sin-forgiven, my gift abuse
Of peace with selfish unconcern?
Has saintly ease no pitying care?
Has faith no work, and love no prayer?
While sin remains, and souls in darkness dwell,
Can heaven itself be heaven, and look unmoved on hell?"

Then through the Gates of Pain, I dream,
A wind of heaven blows coolly in;
Fainter the awful discords seem,
The smoke of torment grows more thin,

Tears quench the burning soil, and thence
Spring sweet, pale flowers of penitence
And through the dreary realm of man's despair,
Star-crowned an angel walks, and to! God's hope is there!

Is it a dream? Is heaven so high
That pity cannot breathe its air?
Its happy eyes forever dry,
Its holy lips without a prayer!
My God! my God! if thither led
By Thy free grace unmerited,
No crown nor palm be mine, but let me keep
A heart that still can feel, and eyes that still can weep.
1868.

THE PRAYER-SEEKER.

Along the aisle where prayer was made,
A woman, all in black arrayed,
Close-veiled, between the kneeling host,
With gliding motion of a ghost,
Passed to the desk, and laid thereon
A scroll which bore these words alone,
  Pray for me!

Back from the place of worshipping
She glided like a guilty thing
The rustle of her draperies, stirred
By hurrying feet, alone was heard;
While, full of awe, the preacher read,
As out into the dark she sped:
  "*Pray for me*!"

Back to the night from whence she came,
To unimagined grief or shame!
Across the threshold of that door
None knew the burden that she bore;
Alone she left the written scroll,
The legend of a troubled soul,--
  Pray for me!

Glide on, poor ghost of woe or sin!
Thou leav'st a common need within;
Each bears, like thee, some nameless weight,
Some misery inarticulate,
Some secret sin, some shrouded dread,
Some household sorrow all unsaid.
***Pray for us*!**

Pass on! The type of all thou art,
Sad witness to the common heart!
With face in veil and seal on lip,
In mute and strange companionship,
Like thee we wander to and fro,
Dumbly imploring as we go
***Pray for us*!**

Ah, who shall pray, since he who pleads
Our want perchance hath greater needs?
Yet they who make their loss the gain
Of others shall not ask in vain,
And Heaven bends low to hear the prayer
Of love from lips of self-despair
***Pray for us*!**

In vain remorse and fear and hate
Beat with bruised bands against a fate
Whose walls of iron only move
And open to the touch of love.
He only feels his burdens fall
Who, taught by suffering, pities all.
***Pray for us*!**

He prayeth best who leaves unguessed

The mystery of another's breast.
Why cheeks grow pale, why eyes o'erflow,
Or heads are white, thou need'st not know.
Enough to note by many a sign
That every heart hath needs like thine.
Pray for us!
1870

THE BREWING OF SOMA.

"These libations mixed with milk have been prepared for Indra:
offer Soma to the drinker of Soma."
--Vashista, translated by MAX MULLER.

The fagots blazed, the caldron's smoke
Up through the green wood curled;
"Bring honey from the hollow oak,
Bring milky sap," the brewers spoke,
In the childhood of the world.

And brewed they well or brewed they ill,
The priests thrust in their rods,
First tasted, and then drank their fill,
And shouted, with one voice and will,
"Behold the drink of gods!"

They drank, and to! in heart and brain
A new, glad life began;
The gray of hair grew young again,
The sick man laughed away his pain,
The cripple leaped and ran.

"Drink, mortals, what the gods have sent,
Forget your long annoy."

So sang the priests. From tent to tent
The Soma's sacred madness went,
A storm of drunken joy.

Then knew each rapt inebriate
A winged and glorious birth,
Soared upward, with strange joy elate,
Beat, with dazed head, Varuna's gate,
And, sobered, sank to earth.

The land with Soma's praises rang;
On Gihon's banks of shade
Its hymns the dusky maidens sang;
In joy of life or mortal pang
All men to Soma prayed.

The morning twilight of the race
Sends down these matin psalms;
And still with wondering eyes we trace
The simple prayers to Soma's grace,
That Vedic verse embalms.

As in that child-world's early year,
Each after age has striven
By music, incense, vigils drear,
And trance, to bring the skies more near,
Or lift men up to heaven!

Some fever of the blood and brain,
Some self-exalting spell,
The scourger's keen delight of pain,
The Dervish dance, the Orphic strain,
The wild-haired Bacchant's yell,--

The desert's hair-grown hermit sunk
The saner brute below;
The naked Santon, hashish-drunk,
The cloister madness of the monk,
The fakir's torture-show!

And yet the past comes round again,
And new doth old fulfil;
In sensual transports wild as vain
We brew in many a Christian fane
The heathen Soma still!

Dear Lord and Father of mankind,
Forgive our foolish ways!
Reclothe us in our rightful mind,
In purer lives Thy service find,
In deeper reverence, praise.

In simple trust like theirs who heard
Beside the Syrian sea
The gracious calling of the Lord,
Let us, like them, without a word,
Rise up and follow Thee.

O Sabbath rest by Galilee!
O calm of hills above,
Where Jesus knelt to share with Thee
The silence of eternity
Interpreted by love!

With that deep hush subduing all
Our words and works that drown
The tender whisper of Thy call,

As noiseless let Thy blessing fall
As fell Thy manna down.

Drop Thy still dews of quietness,
Till all our strivings cease;
Take from our souls the strain and stress,
And let our ordered lives confess
The beauty of Thy peace.

Breathe through the heats of our desire
Thy coolness and Thy balm;
Let sense be dumb, let flesh retire;
Speak through the earthquake, wind, and fire,
O still, small voice of calm!
1872.

A WOMAN.

Oh, dwarfed and wronged, and stained with ill,
Behold! thou art a woman still!
And, by that sacred name and dear,
I bid thy better self appear.
Still, through thy foul disguise, I see
The rudimental purity,
That, spite of change and loss, makes good
Thy birthright-claim of womanhood;
An inward loathing, deep, intense;
A shame that is half innocence.
Cast off the grave-clothes of thy sin!
Rise from the dust thou liest in,
As Mary rose at Jesus' word,
Redeemed and white before the Lord!
Reclaim thy lost soul! In His name,
Rise up, and break thy bonds of shame.
Art weak? He 's strong. Art fearful? Hear
The world's O'ercomer: "Be of cheer!"
What lip shall judge when He approves?
Who dare to scorn the child He loves?

THE PRAYER OF AGASSIZ.

The island of Penikese in Buzzard's Bay was given by Mr. John Anderson to Agassiz for the uses of a summer school of natural history. A large barn was cleared and improvised as a lecture-room. Here, on the first morning of the school, all the company was gathered. "Agassiz had arranged no programme of exercises," says Mrs. Agassiz, in Louis Agassiz; his Life and Correspondence, "trusting to the interest of the occasion to suggest what might best be said or done. But, as he looked upon his pupils gathered there to study nature with him, by an impulse as natural as it was unpremeditated, he called upon then to join in silently asking God's blessing on their work together. The pause was broken by the first words of an address no less fervent than its unspoken prelude." This was in the summer of 1873, and Agassiz died the December following.

On the isle of Penikese,
Ringed about by sapphire seas,
Fanned by breezes salt and cool,
Stood the Master with his school.
Over sails that not in vain
Wooed the west-wind's steady strain,
Line of coast that low and far
Stretched its undulating bar,
Wings aslant along the rim

Of the waves they stooped to skim,
Rock and isle and glistening bay,
Fell the beautiful white day.

Said the Master to the youth
"We have come in search of truth,
Trying with uncertain key
Door by door of mystery;
We are reaching, through His laws,
To the garment-hem of Cause,
Him, the endless, unbegun,
The Unnamable, the One
Light of all our light the Source,
Life of life, and Force of force.
As with fingers of the blind,
We are groping here to find
What the hieroglyphics mean
Of the Unseen in the seen,
What the Thought which underlies
Nature's masking and disguise,
What it is that hides beneath
Blight and bloom and birth and death.
By past efforts unavailing,
Doubt and error, loss and failing,
Of our weakness made aware,
On the threshold of our task
Let us light and guidance ask,
Let us pause in silent prayer!"

Then the Master in his place
Bowed his head a little space,
And the leaves by soft airs stirred,
Lapse of wave and cry of bird,

Left the solemn hush unbroken
Of that wordless prayer unspoken,
While its wish, on earth unsaid,
Rose to heaven interpreted.
As, in life's best hours, we hear
By the spirit's finer ear
His low voice within us, thus
The All-Father heareth us;
And His holy ear we pain
With our noisy words and vain.
Not for Him our violence
Storming at the gates of sense,
His the primal language, His
The eternal silences!

Even the careless heart was moved,
And the doubting gave assent,
With a gesture reverent,
To the Master well-beloved.
As thin mists are glorified
By the light they cannot hide,
All who gazed upon him saw,
Through its veil of tender awe,
How his face was still uplit
By the old sweet look of it.
Hopeful, trustful, full of cheer,
And the love that casts out fear.
Who the secret may declare
Of that brief, unuttered prayer?
Did the shade before him come
Of th' inevitable doom,
Of the end of earth so near,
And Eternity's new year?

In the lap of sheltering seas
Rests the isle of Penikese;
But the lord of the domain
Comes not to his own again
Where the eyes that follow fail,
On a vaster sea his sail
Drifts beyond our beck and hail.
Other lips within its bound
Shall the laws of life expound;
Other eyes from rock and shell
Read the world's old riddles well
But when breezes light and bland
Blow from Summer's blossomed land,
When the air is glad with wings,
And the blithe song-sparrow sings,
Many an eye with his still face
Shall the living ones displace,
Many an ear the word shall seek
He alone could fitly speak.
And one name forevermore
Shall be uttered o'er and o'er
By the waves that kiss the shore,
By the curlew's whistle sent
Down the cool, sea-scented air;
In all voices known to her,
Nature owns her worshipper,
Half in triumph, half lament.
Thither Love shall tearful turn,
Friendship pause uncovered there,
And the wisest reverence learn
From the Master's silent prayer.
1873.

IN QUEST

Have I not voyaged, friend beloved, with thee
On the great waters of the unsounded sea,
Momently listening with suspended oar
For the low rote of waves upon a shore
Changeless as heaven, where never fog-cloud drifts
Over its windless wood, nor mirage lifts
The steadfast hills; where never birds of doubt
Sing to mislead, and every dream dies out,
And the dark riddles which perplex us here
In the sharp solvent of its light are clear?
Thou knowest how vain our quest; how, soon or late,
The baffling tides and circles of debate
Swept back our bark unto its starting-place,
Where, looking forth upon the blank, gray space,
And round about us seeing, with sad eyes,
The same old difficult hills and cloud-cold skies,
We said: "This outward search availeth not
To find Him. He is farther than we thought,
Or, haply, nearer. To this very spot
Whereon we wait, this commonplace of home,
As to the well of Jacob, He may come
And tell us all things." As I listened there,
Through the expectant silences of prayer,
Somewhat I seemed to hear, which hath to me

Been hope, strength, comfort, and I give it thee.

"The riddle of the world is understood
Only by him who feels that God is good,
As only he can feel who makes his love
The ladder of his faith, and climbs above
On th' rounds of his best instincts; draws no line
Between mere human goodness and divine,
But, judging God by what in him is best,
With a child's trust leans on a Father's breast,
And hears unmoved the old creeds babble still
Of kingly power and dread caprice of will,
Chary of blessing, prodigal of curse,
The pitiless doomsman of the universe.
Can Hatred ask for love? Can Selfishness
Invite to self-denial? Is He less
Than man in kindly dealing? Can He break
His own great law of fatherhood, forsake
And curse His children? Not for earth and heaven
Can separate tables of the law be given.
No rule can bind which He himself denies;
The truths of time are not eternal lies."

So heard I; and the chaos round me spread
To light and order grew; and, "Lord," I said,
"Our sins are our tormentors, worst of all
Felt in distrustful shame that dares not call
Upon Thee as our Father. We have set
A strange god up, but Thou remainest yet.
All that I feel of pity Thou hast known
Before I was; my best is all Thy own.
From Thy great heart of goodness mine but drew
Wishes and prayers; but Thou, O Lord, wilt do,

In Thy own time, by ways I cannot see,
All that I feel when I am nearest Thee!"
1873.

THE FRIEND'S BURIAL.

My thoughts are all in yonder town,
Where, wept by many tears,
To-day my mother's friend lays down
The burden of her years.

True as in life, no poor disguise
Of death with her is seen,
And on her simple casket lies
No wreath of bloom and green.

Oh, not for her the florist's art,
The mocking weeds of woe;
Dear memories in each mourner's heart
Like heaven's white lilies blow.

And all about the softening air
Of new-born sweetness tells,
And the ungathered May-flowers wear
The tints of ocean shells.

The old, assuring miracle
Is fresh as heretofore;
And earth takes up its parable
Of life from death once more.

Here organ-swell and church-bell toll
Methinks but discord were;
The prayerful silence of the soul
Is best befitting her.

No sound should break the quietude
Alike of earth and sky
O wandering wind in Seabrook wood,
Breathe but a half-heard sigh!

Sing softly, spring-bird, for her sake;
And thou not distant sea,
Lapse lightly as if Jesus spake,
And thou wert Galilee!

For all her quiet life flowed on
As meadow streamlets flow,
Where fresher green reveals alone
The noiseless ways they go.

From her loved place of prayer I see
The plain-robed mourners pass,
With slow feet treading reverently
The graveyard's springing grass.

Make room, O mourning ones, for me,
Where, like the friends of Paul,
That you no more her face shall see
You sorrow most of all.

Her path shall brighten more and more
Unto the perfect day;
She cannot fail of peace who bore

Such peace with her away.

O sweet, calm face that seemed to wear
The look of sins forgiven!
O voice of prayer that seemed to bear
Our own needs up to heaven!

How reverent in our midst she stood,
Or knelt in grateful praise!
What grace of Christian womanhood
Was in her household ways!

For still her holy living meant
No duty left undone;
The heavenly and the human blent
Their kindred loves in one.

And if her life small leisure found
For feasting ear and eye,
And Pleasure, on her daily round,
She passed unpausing by,

Yet with her went a secret sense
Of all things sweet and fair,
And Beauty's gracious providence
Refreshed her unaware.

She kept her line of rectitude
With love's unconscious ease;
Her kindly instincts understood
All gentle courtesies.

An inborn charm of graciousness

Made sweet her smile and tone,
And glorified her farm-wife dress
With beauty not its own.

The dear Lord's best interpreters
Are humble human souls;
The Gospel of a life like hers
Is more than books or scrolls.

From scheme and creed the light goes out,
The saintly fact survives;
The blessed Master none can doubt
Revealed in holy lives.
1873.

A CHRISTMAS CARMEN.

I.

Sound over all waters, reach out from all lands,
The chorus of voices, the clasping of hands;
Sing hymns that were sung by the stars of the morn,
Sing songs of the angels when Jesus was born!
With glad jubilations
Bring hope to the nations
The dark night is ending and dawn has begun
Rise, hope of the ages, arise like the sun,
All speech flow to music, all hearts beat as one!

II.

Sing the bridal of nations! with chorals of love
Sing out the war-vulture and sing in the dove,
Till the hearts of the peoples keep time in accord,
And the voice of the world is the voice of the Lord!
Clasp hands of the nations
In strong gratulations:
The dark night is ending and dawn has begun;
Rise, hope of the ages, arise like the sun,
All speech flow to music, all hearts beat as one!

III.

Blow, bugles of battle, the marches of peace;

East, west, north, and south let the long quarrel cease
Sing the song of great joy that the angels began,
Sing of glory to God and of good-will to man!
Hark! joining in chorus
The heavens bend o'er us'
The dark night is ending and dawn has begun;
Rise, hope of the ages, arise like the sun,
All speech flow to music, all hearts beat as one!
1873.

VESTA.

O Christ of God! whose life and death
Our own have reconciled,
Most quietly, most tenderly
Take home Thy star-named child!

Thy grace is in her patient eyes,
Thy words are on her tongue;
The very silence round her seems
As if the angels sung.

Her smile is as a listening child's
Who hears its mother call;
The lilies of Thy perfect peace
About her pillow fall.

She leans from out our clinging arms
To rest herself in Thine;
Alone to Thee, dear Lord, can we
Our well-beloved resign!

Oh, less for her than for ourselves
We bow our heads and pray;
Her setting star, like Bethlehem's,
To Thee shall point the way!
1874.

CHILD-SONGS.

Still linger in our noon of time
And on our Saxon tongue
The echoes of the home-born hymns
The Aryan mothers sung.

And childhood had its litanies
In every age and clime;
The earliest cradles of the race
Were rocked to poet's rhyme.

Nor sky, nor wave, nor tree, nor flower,
Nor green earth's virgin sod,
So moved the singer's heart of old
As these small ones of God.

The mystery of unfolding life
Was more than dawning morn,
Than opening flower or crescent moon
The human soul new-born.

And still to childhood's sweet appeal
The heart of genius turns,
And more than all the sages teach
From lisping voices learns,--

The voices loved of him who sang,
Where Tweed and Teviot glide,
That sound to-day on all the winds
That blow from Rydal-side,--

Heard in the Teuton's household songs,
And folk-lore of the Finn,
Where'er to holy Christmas hearths
The Christ-child enters in!

Before life's sweetest mystery still
The heart in reverence kneels;
The wonder of the primal birth
The latest mother feels.

We need love's tender lessons taught
As only weakness can;
God hath His small interpreters;
The child must teach the man.

We wander wide through evil years,
Our eyes of faith grow dim;
But he is freshest from His hands
And nearest unto Him!

And haply, pleading long with Him
For sin-sick hearts and cold,
The angels of our childhood still
The Father's face behold.

Of such the kingdom!--Teach Thou us,
O-Master most divine,
To feel the deep significance

Of these wise words of Thine!

The haughty eye shall seek in vain
What innocence beholds;
No cunning finds the key of heaven,
No strength its gate unfolds.

Alone to guilelessness and love
That gate shall open fall;
The mind of pride is nothingness,
The childlike heart is all!
1875.

THE HEALER.

TO A YOUNG PHYSICIAN, WITH DORE'S PICTURE OF CHRIST
HEALING THE SICK.

So stood of old the holy Christ
Amidst the suffering throng;
With whom His lightest touch sufficed
To make the weakest strong.

That healing gift He lends to them
Who use it in His name;
The power that filled His garment's hem
Is evermore the same.

For lo! in human hearts unseen
The Healer dwelleth still,
And they who make His temples clean
The best subserve His will.

The holiest task by Heaven decreed,
An errand all divine,
The burden of our common need
To render less is thine.

The paths of pain are thine. Go forth
With patience, trust, and hope;

The sufferings of a sin-sick earth
Shall give thee ample scope.

Beside the unveiled mysteries
Of life and death go stand,
With guarded lips and reverent eyes
And pure of heart and hand.

So shalt thou be with power endued
From Him who went about
The Syrian hillsides doing good,
And casting demons out.

That Good Physician liveth yet
Thy friend and guide to be;
The Healer by Gennesaret
Shall walk the rounds with thee.

THE TWO ANGELS.

God called the nearest angels who dwell with Him above:
The tenderest one was Pity, the dearest one was Love.

"Arise," He said, "my angels! a wail of woe and sin
Steals through the gates of heaven, and saddens all within.

"My harps take up the mournful strain that from a lost world swells,
The smoke of torment clouds the light and blights the asphodels.

"Fly downward to that under world, and on its souls of pain
Let Love drop smiles like sunshine, and Pity tears like rain!"

Two faces bowed before the Throne, veiled in their golden hair;
Four white wings lessened swiftly down the dark abyss of air.

The way was strange, the flight was long; at last the angels came
Where swung the lost and nether world, red-wrapped in rayless flame.

There Pity, shuddering, wept; but Love, with faith too strong for fear,
Took heart from God's almightiness and smiled a smile of cheer.

And lo! that tear of Pity quenched the flame whereon it fell,
And, with the sunshine of that smile, hope entered into hell!

Two unveiled faces full of joy looked upward to the Throne,
Four white wings folded at the feet of Him who sat thereon!

And deeper than the sound of seas, more soft than falling flake,
Amidst the hush of wing and song the Voice Eternal spake:

"Welcome, my angels! ye have brought a holier joy to heaven;
Henceforth its sweetest song shall be the song of sin forgiven!"
1875.

OVERRULED.

The threads our hands in blindness spin
No self-determined plan weaves in;
The shuttle of the unseen powers
Works out a pattern not as ours.

Ah! small the choice of him who sings
What sound shall leave the smitten strings;
Fate holds and guides the hand of art;
The singer's is the servant's part.

The wind-harp chooses not the tone
That through its trembling threads is blown;
The patient organ cannot guess
What hand its passive keys shall press.

Through wish, resolve, and act, our will
Is moved by undreamed forces still;
And no man measures in advance
His strength with untried circumstance.

As streams take hue from shade and sun,
As runs the life the song must run;
But, glad or sad, to His good end
God grant the varying notes may tend!
1877.

HYMN OF THE DUNKERS

KLOSTER KEDAR, EPHRATA, PENNSYLVANIA (1738)

SISTER MARIA CHRISTINA sings

Wake, sisters, wake! the day-star shines;
Above Ephrata's eastern pines
The dawn is breaking, cool and calm.
Wake, sisters, wake to prayer and psalm!

Praised be the Lord for shade and light,
For toil by day, for rest by night!
Praised be His name who deigns to bless
Our Kedar of the wilderness!

Our refuge when the spoiler's hand
Was heavy on our native land;
And freedom, to her children due,
The wolf and vulture only knew.

We praised Him when to prison led,
We owned Him when the stake blazed red;
We knew, whatever might befall,
His love and power were over all.

He heard our prayers; with outstretched arm
He led us forth from cruel harm;
Still, wheresoe'er our steps were bent,
His cloud and fire before us went!

The watch of faith and prayer He set,
We kept it then, we keep it yet.
At midnight, crow of cock, or noon,
He cometh sure, He cometh soon.

He comes to chasten, not destroy,
To purge the earth from sin's alloy.
At last, at last shall all confess
His mercy as His righteousness.

The dead shall live, the sick be whole,
The scarlet sin be white as wool;
No discord mar below, above,
The music of eternal love!

Sound, welcome trump, the last alarm!
Lord God of hosts, make bare thine arm,
Fulfil this day our long desire,
Make sweet and clean the world with fire!

Sweep, flaming besom, sweep from sight
The lies of time; be swift to smite,
Sharp sword of God, all idols down,
Genevan creed and Roman crown.

Quake, earth, through all thy zones, till all
The fanes of pride and priestcraft fall;
And lift thou up in place of them

Thy gates of pearl, Jerusalem!

Lo! rising from baptismal flame,
Transfigured, glorious, yet the same,
Within the heavenly city's bound
Our Kloster Kedar shall be found.

He cometh soon! at dawn or noon
Or set of sun, He cometh soon.
Our prayers shall meet Him on His way;
Wake, sisters, wake! arise and pray!
1877.

GIVING AND TAKING.

I have attempted to put in English verse a prose translation of a
poem by Tinnevaluva, a Hindoo poet of the third century of our era.

Who gives and hides the giving hand,
Nor counts on favor, fame, or praise,
Shall find his smallest gift outweighs
The burden of the sea and land.

Who gives to whom hath naught been given,
His gift in need, though small indeed
As is the grass-blade's wind-blown seed,
Is large as earth and rich as heaven.

Forget it not, O man, to whom
A gift shall fall, while yet on earth;
Yea, even to thy seven-fold birth
Recall it in the lives to come.

Who broods above a wrong in thought
Sins much; but greater sin is his
Who, fed and clothed with kindnesses,
Shall count the holy alms as nought.

Who dares to curse the hands that bless

Shall know of sin the deadliest cost;
The patience of the heavens is lost
Beholding man's unthankfulness.

For he who breaks all laws may still
In Sivam's mercy be forgiven;
But none can save, in earth or heaven,
The wretch who answers good with ill.
1877.

THE VISION OF ECHARD.

The Benedictine Echard
Sat by the wayside well,
Where Marsberg sees the bridal
Of the Sarre and the Moselle.

Fair with its sloping vineyards
And tawny chestnut bloom,
The happy vale Ausonius sunk
For holy Treves made room.

On the shrine Helena builded
To keep the Christ coat well,
On minster tower and kloster cross,
The westering sunshine fell.

There, where the rock-hewn circles
O'erlooked the Roman's game,
The veil of sleep fell on him,
And his thought a dream became.

He felt the heart of silence
Throb with a soundless word,
And by the inward ear alone
A spirit's voice he heard.

And the spoken word seemed written
On air and wave and sod,
And the bending walls of sapphire
Blazed with the thought of God.

"What lack I, O my children?
All things are in my band;
The vast earth and the awful stars
I hold as grains of sand.

"Need I your alms? The silver
And gold are mine alone;
The gifts ye bring before me
Were evermore my own.

"Heed I the noise of viols,
Your pomp of masque and show?
Have I not dawns and sunsets
Have I not winds that blow?

"Do I smell your gums of incense?
Is my ear with chantings fed?
Taste I your wine of worship,
Or eat your holy bread?

"Of rank and name and honors
Am I vain as ye are vain?
What can Eternal Fulness
From your lip-service gain?

"Ye make me not your debtor
Who serve yourselves alone;
Ye boast to me of homage

Whose gain is all your own.

"For you I gave the prophets,
For you the Psalmist's lay
For you the law's stone tables,
And holy book and day.

"Ye change to weary burdens
The helps that should uplift;
Ye lose in form the spirit,
The Giver in the gift.

"Who called ye to self-torment,
To fast and penance vain?
Dream ye Eternal Goodness
Has joy in mortal pain?

"For the death in life of Nitria,
For your Chartreuse ever dumb,
What better is the neighbor,
Or happier the home?

"Who counts his brother's welfare
As sacred as his own,
And loves, forgives, and pities,
He serveth me alone.

"I note each gracious purpose,
Each kindly word and deed;
Are ye not all my children?
Shall not the Father heed?

"No prayer for light and guidance
Is lost upon mine ear
The child's cry in the darkness
Shall not the Father hear?

"I loathe your wrangling councils,
I tread upon your creeds;
Who made ye mine avengers,
Or told ye of my needs;

"I bless men and ye curse them,
I love them and ye hate;
Ye bite and tear each other,
I suffer long and wait.

"Ye bow to ghastly symbols,
To cross and scourge and thorn;
Ye seek his Syrian manger
Who in the heart is born.

"For the dead Christ, not the living,
Ye watch His empty grave,
Whose life alone within you
Has power to bless and save.

"O blind ones, outward groping,
The idle quest forego;
Who listens to His inward voice
Alone of Him shall know.

"His love all love exceeding
The heart must needs recall,
Its self-surrendering freedom,

Its loss that gaineth all.

"Climb not the holy mountains,
Their eagles know not me;
Seek not the Blessed Islands,
I dwell not in the sea.

"Gone is the mount of Meru,
The triple gods are gone,
And, deaf to all the lama's prayers,
The Buddha slumbers on.

"No more from rocky Horeb
The smitten waters gush;
Fallen is Bethel's ladder,
Quenched is the burning bush.

"The jewels of the Urim
And Thurnmim all are dim;
The fire has left the altar,
The sign the teraphim.

"No more in ark or hill grove
The Holiest abides;
Not in the scroll's dead letter
The eternal secret hides.

"The eye shall fail that searches
For me the hollow sky;
The far is even as the near,
The low is as the high.

"What if the earth is hiding
Her old faiths, long outworn?
What is it to the changeless truth
That yours shall fail in turn?

"What if the o'erturned altar
Lays bare the ancient lie?
What if the dreams and legends
Of the world's childhood die?

"Have ye not still my witness
Within yourselves alway,
My hand that on the keys of life
For bliss or bale I lay?

"Still, in perpetual judgment,
I hold assize within,
With sure reward of holiness,
And dread rebuke of sin.

"A light, a guide, a warning,
A presence ever near,
Through the deep silence of the flesh
I reach the inward ear.

"My Gerizim and Ebal
Are in each human soul,
The still, small voice of blessing,
And Sinai's thunder-roll.

"The stern behest of duty,
The doom-book open thrown,
The heaven ye seek, the hell ye fear,

Are with yourselves alone."

. . . . .

A gold and purple sunset
Flowed down the broad Moselle;
On hills of vine and meadow lands
The peace of twilight fell.

A slow, cool wind of evening
Blew over leaf and bloom;
And, faint and far, the Angelus
Rang from Saint Matthew's tomb.

Then up rose Master Echard,
And marvelled: "Can it be
That here, in dream and vision,
The Lord hath talked with me?"

He went his way; behind him
The shrines of saintly dead,
The holy coat and nail of cross,
He left unvisited.

He sought the vale of Eltzbach
His burdened soul to free,
Where the foot-hills of the Eifel
Are glassed in Laachersee.

And, in his Order's kloster,
He sat, in night-long parle,
With Tauler of the Friends of God,
And Nicolas of Basle.

And lo! the twain made answer
"Yea, brother, even thus
The Voice above all voices
Hath spoken unto us.

"The world will have its idols,
And flesh and sense their sign
But the blinded eyes shall open,
And the gross ear be fine.

"What if the vision tarry?
God's time is always best;
The true Light shall be witnessed,
The Christ within confessed.

"In mercy or in judgment
He shall turn and overturn,
Till the heart shall be His temple
Where all of Him shall learn."

INSCRIPTIONS.

ON A SUN-DIAL.

FOR DR. HENRY I. BOWDITCH.

With warning hand I mark Time's rapid flight
From life's glad morning to its solemn night;
Yet, through the dear God's love, I also show
There's Light above me by the Shade below.
1879.

ON A FOUNTAIN.

FOR DOROTHEA L. DIX.

Stranger and traveller,
Drink freely and bestow
A kindly thought on her
Who bade this fountain flow,
Yet hath no other claim
Than as the minister
Of blessing in God's name.
Drink, and in His peace go
1879

THE MINISTER'S DAUGHTER.

In the minister's morning sermon
He had told of the primal fall,
And how thenceforth the wrath of God
Rested on each and all.

And how of His will and pleasure,
All souls, save a chosen few,
Were doomed to the quenchless burning,
And held in the way thereto.

Yet never by faith's unreason
A saintlier soul was tried,
And never the harsh old lesson
A tenderer heart belied.

And, after the painful service
On that pleasant Sabbath day,
He walked with his little daughter
Through the apple-bloom of May.

Sweet in the fresh green meadows
Sparrow and blackbird sung;
Above him their tinted petals
The blossoming orchards hung.

Around on the wonderful glory
The minister looked and smiled;
"How good is the Lord who gives us
These gifts from His hand, my child.

"Behold in the bloom of apples
And the violets in the sward
A hint of the old, lost beauty
Of the Garden of the Lord!"

Then up spake the little maiden,
Treading on snow and pink
"O father! these pretty blossoms
Are very wicked, I think.

"Had there been no Garden of Eden
There never had been a fall;
And if never a tree had blossomed
God would have loved us all."

"Hush, child!" the father answered,
"By His decree man fell;
His ways are in clouds and darkness,
But He doeth all things well.

"And whether by His ordaining
To us cometh good or ill,
Joy or pain, or light or shadow,
We must fear and love Him still."

"Oh, I fear Him!" said the daughter,
"And I try to love Him, too;
But I wish He was good and gentle,

Kind and loving as you."

The minister groaned in spirit
As the tremulous lips of pain
And wide, wet eyes uplifted
Questioned his own in vain.

Bowing his head he pondered
The words of the little one;
Had he erred in his life-long teaching?
Had he wrong to his Master done?

To what grim and dreadful idol
Had he lent the holiest name?
Did his own heart, loving and human,
The God of his worship shame?

And lo! from the bloom and greenness,
From the tender skies above,
And the face of his little daughter,
He read a lesson of love.

No more as the cloudy terror
Of Sinai's mount of law,
But as Christ in the Syrian lilies
The vision of God he saw.

And, as when, in the clefts of Horeb,
Of old was His presence known,
The dread Ineffable Glory
Was Infinite Goodness alone.

Thereafter his hearers noted
In his prayers a tenderer strain,
And never the gospel of hatred
Burned on his lips again.

And the scoffing tongue was prayerful,
And the blinded eyes found sight,
And hearts, as flint aforetime,
Grew soft in his warmth and light.
1880.

BY THEIR WORKS.

Call him not heretic whose works attest
His faith in goodness by no creed confessed.
Whatever in love's name is truly done
To free the bound and lift the fallen one
Is done to Christ. Whoso in deed and word
Is not against Him labors for our Lord.
When He, who, sad and weary, longing sore
For love's sweet service, sought the sisters' door,
One saw the heavenly, one the human guest,
But who shall say which loved the Master best?
1881.

THE WORD.

Voice of the Holy Spirit, making known
Man to himself, a witness swift and sure,
Warning, approving, true and wise and pure,
Counsel and guidance that misleadeth none!
By thee the mystery of life is read;
The picture-writing of the world's gray seers,
The myths and parables of the primal years,
Whose letter kills, by thee interpreted
Take healthful meanings fitted to our needs,
And in the soul's vernacular express
The common law of simple righteousness.
Hatred of cant and doubt of human creeds
May well be felt: the unpardonable sin
Is to deny the Word of God within!
1881.

THE BOOK.

Gallery of sacred pictures manifold,
A minster rich in holy effigies,
And bearing on entablature and frieze
The hieroglyphic oracles of old.
Along its transept aureoled martyrs sit;
And the low chancel side-lights half acquaint
The eye with shrines of prophet, bard, and saint,
Their age-dimmed tablets traced in doubtful writ!
But only when on form and word obscure
Falls from above the white supernal light
We read the mystic characters aright,
And life informs the silent portraiture,
Until we pause at last, awe-held, before
The One ineffable Face, love, wonder, and adore.
1881

REQUIREMENT.

We live by Faith; but Faith is not the slave
Of text and legend. Reason's voice and God's,
Nature's and Duty's, never are at odds.
What asks our Father of His children, save
Justice and mercy and humility,
A reasonable service of good deeds,
Pure living, tenderness to human needs,
Reverence and trust, and prayer for light to see
The Master's footprints in our daily ways?
No knotted scourge nor sacrificial knife,
But the calm beauty of an ordered life
Whose very breathing is unworded praise!--
A life that stands as all true lives have stood,
Firm-rooted in the faith that God is Good.
1881.

HELP.

Dream not, O Soul, that easy is the task
Thus set before thee. If it proves at length,
As well it may, beyond thy natural strength,
Faint not, despair not. As a child may ask
A father, pray the Everlasting Good
For light and guidance midst the subtle snares
Of sin thick planted in life's thoroughfares,
For spiritual strength and moral hardihood;
Still listening, through the noise of time and sense,
To the still whisper of the Inward Word;
Bitter in blame, sweet in approval heard,
Itself its own confirming evidence
To health of soul a voice to cheer and please,
To guilt the wrath of the Eumenides.
1881.

UTTERANCE.

But what avail inadequate words to reach
The innermost of Truth? Who shall essay,
Blinded and weak, to point and lead the way,
Or solve the mystery in familiar speech?
Yet, if it be that something not thy own,
Some shadow of the Thought to which our schemes,
Creeds, cult, and ritual are at best but dreams,
Is even to thy unworthiness made known,
Thou mayst not hide what yet thou shouldst not dare
To utter lightly, lest on lips of thine
The real seem false, the beauty undivine.
So, weighing duty in the scale of prayer,
Give what seems given thee. It may prove a seed
Of goodness dropped in fallow-grounds of need.
1881.

ORIENTAL MAXIMS.

PARAPHRASE OF SANSCRIT TRANSLATIONS.

THE INWARD JUDGE.

From Institutes of Manu.

The soul itself its awful witness is.
Say not in evil doing, "No one sees,"
And so offend the conscious One within,
Whose ear can hear the silences of sin.

Ere they find voice, whose eyes unsleeping see
The secret motions of iniquity.
Nor in thy folly say, "I am alone."
For, seated in thy heart, as on a throne,
The ancient Judge and Witness liveth still,
To note thy act and thought; and as thy ill
Or good goes from thee, far beyond thy reach,
The solemn Doomsman's seal is set on each.
1878.

LAYING UP TREASURE

From the Mahabharata.

Before the Ender comes, whose charioteer
Is swift or slow Disease, lay up each year
Thy harvests of well-doing, wealth that kings
Nor thieves can take away. When all the things
Thou tallest thine, goods, pleasures, honors fall,
Thou in thy virtue shalt survive them all.
1881.

CONDUCT

From the Mahabharata.

Heed how thou livest. Do no act by day
Which from the night shall drive thy peace away.
In months of sun so live that months of rain
Shall still be happy. Evermore restrain
Evil and cherish good, so shall there be
Another and a happier life for thee.
1881.

AN EASTER FLOWER GIFT.

O dearest bloom the seasons know,
Flowers of the Resurrection blow,
Our hope and faith restore;
And through the bitterness of death
And loss and sorrow, breathe a breath
Of life forevermore!

The thought of Love Immortal blends
With fond remembrances of friends;
In you, O sacred flowers,
By human love made doubly sweet,
The heavenly and the earthly meet,
The heart of Christ and ours!
1882.

THE MYSTIC'S CHRISTMAS.

"All hail!" the bells of Christmas rang,
"All hail!" the monks at Christmas sang,
The merry monks who kept with cheer
The gladdest day of all their year.

But still apart, unmoved thereat,
A pious elder brother sat
Silent, in his accustomed place,
With God's sweet peace upon his face.

"Why sitt'st thou thus?" his brethren cried.
"It is the blessed Christmas-tide;
The Christmas lights are all aglow,
The sacred lilies bud and blow.

"Above our heads the joy-bells ring,
Without the happy children sing,
And all God's creatures hail the morn
On which the holy Christ was born!

"Rejoice with us; no more rebuke
Our gladness with thy quiet look."
The gray monk answered: "Keep, I pray,
Even as ye list, the Lord's birthday.

"Let heathen Yule fires flicker red
Where thronged refectory feasts are spread;
With mystery-play and masque and mime
And wait-songs speed the holy time!

"The blindest faith may haply save;
The Lord accepts the things we have;
And reverence, howsoe'er it strays,
May find at last the shining ways.

"They needs must grope who cannot see,
The blade before the ear must be;
As ye are feeling I have felt,
And where ye dwell I too have dwelt.

"But now, beyond the things of sense,
Beyond occasions and events,
I know, through God's exceeding grace,
Release from form and time and place.

"I listen, from no mortal tongue,
To hear the song the angels sung;
And wait within myself to know
The Christmas lilies bud and blow.

"The outward symbols disappear
From him whose inward sight is clear;
And small must be the choice of clays
To him who fills them all with praise!

"Keep while you need it, brothers mine,
With honest zeal your Christmas sign,
But judge not him who every morn

Feels in his heart the Lord Christ born!"
1882.

AT LAST.

When on my day of life the night is falling,
And, in the winds from unsunned spaces blown,
I hear far voices out of darkness calling
My feet to paths unknown,

Thou who hast made my home of life so pleasant,
Leave not its tenant when its walls decay;
O Love Divine, O Helper ever present,
Be Thou my strength and stay!

Be near me when all else is from me drifting
Earth, sky, home's pictures, days of shade and shine,
And kindly faces to my own uplifting
The love which answers mine.

I have but Thee, my Father! let Thy spirit
Be with me then to comfort and uphold;
No gate of pearl, no branch of palm I merit,
Nor street of shining gold.

Suffice it if--my good and ill unreckoned,
And both forgiven through Thy abounding grace--
I find myself by hands familiar beckoned
Unto my fitting place.

Some humble door among Thy many mansions,
Some sheltering shade where sin and striving cease,
And flows forever through heaven's green expansions
The river of Thy peace.

There, from the music round about me stealing,
I fain would learn the new and holy song,
And find at last, beneath Thy trees of healing,
The life for which I long.
1882

WHAT THE TRAVELLER SAID AT SUNSET.

The shadows grow and deepen round me,
I feel the deffall in the air;
The muezzin of the darkening thicket,
I hear the night-thrush call to prayer.

The evening wind is sad with farewells,
And loving hands unclasp from mine;
Alone I go to meet the darkness
Across an awful boundary-line.

As from the lighted hearths behind me
I pass with slow, reluctant feet,
What waits me in the land of strangeness?
What face shall smile, what voice shall greet?

What space shall awe, what brightness blind me?
What thunder-roll of music stun?
What vast processions sweep before me
Of shapes unknown beneath the sun?

I shrink from unaccustomed glory,
I dread the myriad-voiced strain;
Give me the unforgotten faces,
And let my lost ones speak again.

He will not chide my mortal yearning
Who is our Brother and our Friend;
In whose full life, divine and human,
The heavenly and the earthly blend.

Mine be the joy of soul-communion,
The sense of spiritual strength renewed,
The reverence for the pure and holy,
The dear delight of doing good.

No fitting ear is mine to listen
An endless anthem's rise and fall;
No curious eye is mine to measure
The pearl gate and the jasper wall.

For love must needs be more than knowledge:
What matter if I never know
Why Aldebaran's star is ruddy,
Or warmer Sirius white as snow!

Forgive my human words, O Father!
I go Thy larger truth to prove;
Thy mercy shall transcend my longing
I seek but love, and Thou art Love!

I go to find my lost and mourned for
Safe in Thy sheltering goodness still,
And all that hope and faith foreshadow
Made perfect in Thy holy will!
1883.

THE "STORY OF IDA."

Francesca Alexander, whose pen and pencil have so reverently
transcribed the simple faith and life of the Italian peasantry,
wrote the narrative published with John Ruskin's introduction under
the title, *The Story of Ida*.

Weary of jangling noises never stilled,
The skeptic's sneer, the bigot's hate, the din
Of clashing texts, the webs of creed men spin
Round simple truth, the children grown who build
With gilded cards their new Jerusalem,
Busy, with sacerdotal tailorings
And tinsel gauds, bedizening holy things,
I turn, with glad and grateful heart, from them
To the sweet story of the Florentine
Immortal in her blameless maidenhood,
Beautiful as God's angels and as good;
Feeling that life, even now, may be divine
With love no wrong can ever change to hate,
No sin make less than all-compassionate!
1884.

THE LIGHT THAT IS FELT.

A tender child of summers three,
Seeking her little bed at night,
Paused on the dark stair timidly.
"Oh, mother! Take my hand," said she,
"And then the dark will all be light."

We older children grope our way
From dark behind to dark before;
And only when our hands we lay,
Dear Lord, in Thine, the night is day,
And there is darkness nevermore.

Reach downward to the sunless days
Wherein our guides are blind as we,
And faith is small and hope delays;
Take Thou the hands of prayer we raise,
And let us feel the light of Thee!
1884.

THE TWO LOVES

Smoothing soft the nestling head
Of a maiden fancy-led,
Thus a grave-eyed woman said:

"Richest gifts are those we make,
Dearer than the love we take
That we give for love's own sake.

"Well I know the heart's unrest;
Mine has been the common quest,
To be loved and therefore blest.

"Favors undeserved were mine;
At my feet as on a shrine
Love has laid its gifts divine.

"Sweet the offerings seemed, and yet
With their sweetness came regret,
And a sense of unpaid debt.

"Heart of mine unsatisfied,
Was it vanity or pride
That a deeper joy denied?

"Hands that ope but to receive
Empty close; they only live
Richly who can richly give.

"Still," she sighed, with moistening eyes,
"Love is sweet in any guise;
But its best is sacrifice!

"He who, giving, does not crave
Likest is to Him who gave
Life itself the loved to save.

"Love, that self-forgetful gives,
Sows surprise of ripened sheaves,
Late or soon its own receives."
1884.

ADJUSTMENT.

The tree of Faith its bare, dry boughs must shed
That nearer heaven the living ones may climb;
The false must fail, though from our shores of time
The old lament be heard, "Great Pan is dead!"
That wail is Error's, from his high place hurled;
This sharp recoil is Evil undertrod;
Our time's unrest, an angel sent of God
Troubling with life the waters of the world.
Even as they list the winds of the Spirit blow
To turn or break our century-rusted vanes;
Sands shift and waste; the rock alone remains
Where, led of Heaven, the strong tides come and go,
And storm-clouds, rent by thunderbolt and wind,
Leave, free of mist, the permanent stars behind.

Therefore I trust, although to outward sense
Both true and false seem shaken; I will hold
With newer light my reverence for the old,
And calmly wait the births of Providence.
No gain is lost; the clear-eyed saints look down
Untroubled on the wreck of schemes and creeds;
Love yet remains, its rosary of good deeds
Counting in task-field and o'erpeopled town;
Truth has charmed life; the Inward Word survives,

And, day by day, its revelation brings;
Faith, hope, and charity, whatsoever things
Which cannot be shaken, stand. Still holy lives
Reveal the Christ of whom the letter told,
And the new gospel verifies the old.
1885.

HYMNS OF THE BRAHMO SOMAJ.

I have attempted this paraphrase of the Hymns of the Brahmo Somaj of India, as I find them in Mozoomdar's account of the devotional exercises of that remarkable religious development which has attracted far less attention and sympathy from the Christian world than it deserves, as a fresh revelation of the direct action of the Divine Spirit upon the human heart.

I.
The mercy, O Eternal One!
By man unmeasured yet,
In joy or grief, in shade or sun,
I never will forget.
I give the whole, and not a part,
Of all Thou gayest me;
My goods, my life, my soul and heart,
I yield them all to Thee!

II.
We fast and plead, we weep and pray,
From morning until even;
We feel to find the holy way,
We knock at the gate of heaven
And when in silent awe we wait,
And word and sign forbear,
The hinges of the golden gate

Move, soundless, to our prayer!
Who hears the eternal harmonies
Can heed no outward word;
Blind to all else is he who sees
The vision of the Lord!

III.
O soul, be patient, restrain thy tears,
Have hope, and not despair;
As a tender mother heareth her child
God hears the penitent prayer.
And not forever shall grief be thine;
On the Heavenly Mother's breast,
Washed clean and white in the waters of joy
Shall His seeking child find rest.
Console thyself with His word of grace,
And cease thy wail of woe,
For His mercy never an equal hath,
And His love no bounds can know.
Lean close unto Him in faith and hope;
How many like thee have found
In Him a shelter and home of peace,
By His mercy compassed round!
There, safe from sin and the sorrow it brings,
They sing their grateful psalms,
And rest, at noon, by the wells of God,
In the shade of His holy palms!
1885.

REVELATION.

"And I went into the Vale of Beavor, and as I went I preached repentance to the people. And one morning, sitting by the fire, a great cloud came over me, and a temptation beset me. And it was said: All things come by Nature; and the Elements and the Stars came over me. And as I sat still and let it alone, a living hope arose in me, and a true Voice which said: There is a living God who made all things. And immediately the cloud and the temptation vanished, and Life rose over all, and my heart was glad and I praised the Living God."--Journal of George Fox,
1690.

Still, as of old, in Beavor's Vale,
O man of God! our hope and faith
The Elements and Stars assail,
And the awed spirit holds its breath,
Blown over by a wind of death.

Takes Nature thought for such as we,
What place her human atom fills,
The weed-drift of her careless sea,
The mist on her unheeding hills?
What reeks she of our helpless wills?

Strange god of Force, with fear, not love,
Its trembling worshipper! Can prayer

Reach the shut ear of Fate, or move
Unpitying Energy to spare?
What doth the cosmic Vastness care?

In vain to this dread Unconcern
For the All-Father's love we look;
In vain, in quest of it, we turn
The storied leaves of Nature's book,
The prints her rocky tablets took.

I pray for faith, I long to trust;
I listen with my heart, and hear
A Voice without a sound: "Be just,
Be true, be merciful, revere
The Word within thee: God is near!

"A light to sky and earth unknown
Pales all their lights: a mightier force
Than theirs the powers of Nature own,
And, to its goal as at its source,
His Spirit moves the Universe.

"Believe and trust. Through stars and suns,
Through life and death, through soul and sense,
His wise, paternal purpose runs;
The darkness of His providence
Is star-lit with benign intents."

O joy supreme! I know the Voice,
Like none beside on earth or sea;
Yea, more, O soul of mine, rejoice,
By all that He requires of me,
I know what God himself must be.

No picture to my aid I call,
I shape no image in my prayer;
I only know in Him is all
Of life, light, beauty, everywhere,
Eternal Goodness here and there!

I know He is, and what He is,
Whose one great purpose is the good
Of all. I rest my soul on His
Immortal Love and Fatherhood;
And trust Him, as His children should.

I fear no more. The clouded face
Of Nature smiles; through all her things
Of time and space and sense I trace
The moving of the Spirit's wings,
And hear the song of hope she sings.
1886

The Codes Of Hammurabi And Moses
W. W. Davies

The discovery of the Hammurabi Code is one of the greatest achievements of archaeology, and is of paramount interest, not only to the student of the Bible, but also to all those interested in ancient history...

Religion   **ISBN:** *1-59462-338-4*   Pages:132
MSRP $12.95

QTY

The Theory of Moral Sentiments
Adam Smith

This work from 1749. contains original theories of conscience amd moral judgment and it is the foundation for systemof morals.

Philosophy **ISBN:** *1-59462-777-0*   Pages:536
MSRP $19.95

QTY

Jessica's First Prayer
Hesba Stretton

In a screened and secluded corner of one of the many railway-bridges which span the streets of London there could be seen a few years ago, from five o'clock every morning until half past eight, a tidily set-out coffee-stall, consisting of a trestle and board, upon which stood two large tin cans, with a small fire of charcoal burning under each so as to keep the coffee boiling during the early hours of the morning when the work-people were thronging into the city on their way to their daily toil...

Childrens   **ISBN:** *1-59462-373-2*   Pages:84
MSRP $9.95

QTY

My Life and Work
Henry Ford

Henry Ford revolutionized the world with his implementation of mass production for the Model T automobile. Gain valuable business insight into his life and work with his own auto-biography... "We have only started on our development of our country we have not as yet, with all our talk of wonderful progress, done more than scratch the surface. The progress has been wonderful enough but..."

Biographies/   **ISBN:** *1-59462-198-5*   Pages:300
MSRP $21.95

QTY

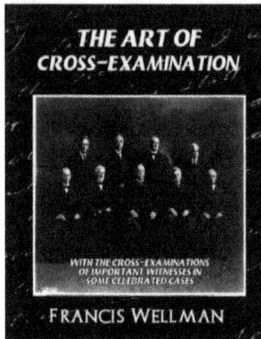

The Art of Cross-Examination
Francis Wellman

QTY

I presume it is the experience of every author, after his first book is published upon an important subject, to be almost overwhelmed with a wealth of ideas and illustrations which could readily have been included in his book, and which to his own mind, at least, seem to make a second edition inevitable. Such certainly was the case with me; and when the first edition had reached its sixth impression in five months, I rejoiced to learn that it seemed to my publishers that the book had met with a sufficiently favorable reception to justify a second and considerably enlarged edition. ..

Reference   ISBN: *1-59462-647-2*

Pages:412

MSRP $19.95

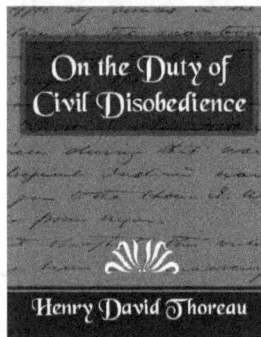

On the Duty of Civil Disobedience
Henry David Thoreau

QTY

Thoreau wrote his famous essay, On the Duty of Civil Disobedience, as a protest against an unjust but popular war and the immoral but popular institution of slave-owning. He did more than write—he declined to pay his taxes, and was hauled off to gaol in consequence. Who can say how much this refusal of his hastened the end of the war and of slavery ?

Law   ISBN: *1-59462-747-9*

Pages:48

MSRP $7.45

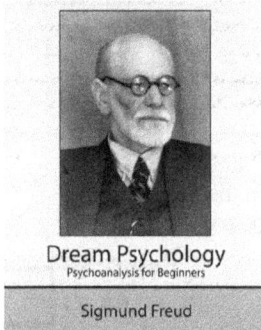

Dream Psychology Psychoanalysis for Beginners
Sigmund Freud

QTY

Sigmund Freud, born Sigismund Schlomo Freud (May 6, 1856 - September 23, 1939), was a Jewish-Austrian neurologist and psychiatrist who co-founded the psychoanalytic school of psychology. Freud is best known for his theories of the unconscious mind, especially involving the mechanism of repression; his redefinition of sexual desire as mobile and directed towards a wide variety of objects; and his therapeutic techniques, especially his understanding of transference in the therapeutic relationship and the presumed value of dreams as sources of insight into unconscious desires.

Psychology   ISBN: *1-59462-905-6*

Pages:196

MSRP $15.45

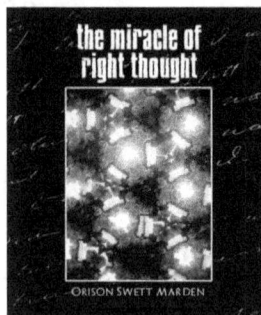

The Miracle of Right Thought
Orison Swett Marden

QTY

Believe with all of your heart that you will do what you were made to do. When the mind has once formed the habit of holding cheerful, happy, prosperous pictures, it will not be easy to form the opposite habit. It does not matter how improbable or how far away this realization may see, or how dark the prospects may be, if we visualize them as best we can, as vividly as possible, hold tenaciously to them and vigorously struggle to attain them, they will gradually become actualized, realized in the life. But a desire, a longing without endeavor, a yearning abandoned or held indifferently will vanish without realization.

Pages:360

Self Help   ISBN: *1-59462-644-8*

MSRP $25.45

www.bookjungle.com *email: sales@bookjungle.com fax: 630-214-0564 mail: Book Jungle PO Box 2226 Champaign, IL 61825*

QTY

The Rosicrucian Cosmo-Conception Mystic Christianity *by Max Heindel* ISBN: *1-59462-188-8* **$38.95**
The Rosicrucian Cosmo-conception is not dogmatic, neither does it appeal to any other authority than the reason of the student. It is: not controversial, but is: sent forth in the, hope that it may help to clear.. New Age/Religion Pages 646

Abandonment To Divine Providence *by Jean-Pierre de Caussade* ISBN: *1-59462-228-0* **$25.95**
"The Rev. Jean Pierre de Caussade was one of the most remarkable spiritual writers of the Society of Jesus in France in the 18th Century. His death took place at Toulouse in 1751. His works have gone through many editions and have been republished... Inspirational/Religion Pages 400

Mental Chemistry *by Charles Haanel* ISBN: *1-59462-192-6* **$23.95**
Mental Chemistry allows the change of material conditions by combining and appropriately utilizing the power of the mind. Much like applied chemistry creates something new and unique out of careful combinations of chemicals the mastery of mental chemistry... New Age Pages 354

The Letters of Robert Browning and Elizabeth Barret Barrett 1845-1846 vol II ISBN: *1-59462-193-4* **$35.95**
by Robert Browning and Elizabeth Barrett Biographies Pages 596

Gleanings In Genesis (volume I) *by Arthur W. Pink* ISBN: *1-59462-130-6* **$27.45**
Appropriately has Genesis been termed "the seed plot of the Bible" for in it we have, in germ form, almost all of the great doctrines which are afterwards fully developed in the books of Scripture which follow... Religion/Inspirational Pages 420

The Master Key *by L. W. de Laurence* ISBN: *1-59462-001-6* **$30.95**
In no branch of human knowledge has there been a more lively increase of the spirit of research during the past few years than in the study of Psychology, Concentration and Mental Discipline. The requests for authentic lessons in Thought Control, Mental Discipline and... New Age/Business Pages 422

The Lesser Key Of Solomon Goetia *by L. W. de Laurence* ISBN: *1-59462-092-X* **$9.95**
This translation of the first book of the "Lernegton" which is now for the first time made accessible to students of Talismanic Magic was done, after careful collation and edition, from numerous Ancient Manuscripts in Hebrew, Latin, and French... New Age/Occult Pages 92

Rubaiyat Of Omar Khayyam *by Edward Fitzgerald* ISBN:*1-59462-332-5* **$13.95**
Edward Fitzgerald, whom the world has already learned, in spite of his own efforts to remain within the shadow of anonymity, to look upon as one of the rarest poets of the century, was born at Bredfield, in Suffolk, on the 31st of March, 1809. He was the third son of John Purcell... Music Pages 172

Ancient Law *by Henry Maine* ISBN: *1-59462-128-4* **$29.95**
The chief object of the following pages is to indicate some of the earliest ideas of mankind, as they are reflected in Ancient Law, and to point out the relation of those ideas to modern thought. Religiom/History Pages 452

Far-Away Stories *by William J. Locke* ISBN: *1-59462-129-2* **$19.45**
"Good wine needs no bush, but a collection of mixed vintages does. And this book is just such a collection. Some of the stories I do not want to remain buried for ever in the museum files of dead magazine-numbers an author's not unpardonable vanity..." Fiction Pages 272

Life of David Crockett *by David Crockett* ISBN: *1-59462-250-7* **$27.45**
"Colonel David Crockett was one of the most remarkable men of the times in which he lived. Born in humble life, but gifted with a strong will, an indomitable courage, and unremitting perseverance... Biographies/New Age Pages 424

Lip-Reading *by Edward Nitchie* ISBN: *1-59462-206-X* **$25.95**
Edward B. Nitchie, founder of the New York School for the Hard of Hearing, now the Nitchie School of Lip-Reading, Inc, wrote "LIP-READING Principles and Practice". The development and perfecting of this meritorious work on lip-reading was an undertaking... How-to Pages 400

A Handbook of Suggestive Therapeutics, Applied Hypnotism, Psychic Science ISBN: *1-59462-214-0* **$24.95**
by Henry Munro Health/New Age/Health/Self-help Pages 376

A Doll's House: and Two Other Plays *by Henrik Ibsen* ISBN: *1-59462-112-8* **$19.95**
Henrik Ibsen created this classic when in revolutionary 1848 Rome. Introducing some striking concepts in playwriting for the realist genre, this play has been studied the world over. Fiction/Classics/Plays 308

The Light of Asia *by sir Edwin Arnold* ISBN: *1-59462-204-3* **$13.95**
In this poetic masterpiece, Edwin Arnold describes the life and teachings of Buddha. The man who was to become known as Buddha to the world was born as Prince Gautama of India but he rejected the worldly riches and abandoned the reigns of power when... Religion/History/Biographies Pages 170

The Complete Works of Guy de Maupassant *by Guy de Maupassant* ISBN: *1-59462-157-8* **$16.95**
"For days and days, nights and nights, I had dreamed of that first kiss which was to consecrate our engagement, and I knew not on what spot I should put my lips..." Fiction/Classics Pages 240

The Art of Cross-Examination *by Francis L. Wellman* ISBN: *1-59462-309-0* **$26.95**
Written by a renowned trial lawyer, Wellman imparts his experience and uses case studies to explain how to use psychology to extract desired information through questioning. How-to/Science/Reference Pages 408

Answered or Unanswered? *by Louisa Vaughan* ISBN: *1-59462-248-5* **$10.95**
Miracles of Faith in China Religion Pages 112

The Edinburgh Lectures on Mental Science (1909) *by Thomas* ISBN: *1-59462-008-3* **$11.95**
This book contains the substance of a course of lectures recently given by the writer in the Queen Street Hail, Edinburgh. Its purpose is to indicate the Natural Principles governing the relation between Mental Action and Material Conditions... New Age/Psychology Pages 148

Ayesha *by H. Rider Haggard* ISBN: *1-59462-301-5* **$24.95**
Verily and indeed it is the unexpected that happens! Probably if there was one person upon the earth from whom the Editor of this, and of a certain previous history, did not expect to hear again... Classics Pages 380

Ayala's Angel *by Anthony Trollope* ISBN: *1-59462-352-X* **$29.95**
The two girls were both pretty, but Lucy who was twenty-one who supposed to be simple and comparatively unattractive, whereas Ayala was credited, as her Bombwhat romantic name might show, with poetic charm and a taste for romance. Ayala when her father died was nineteen... Fiction Pages 484

The American Commonwealth *by James Bryce* ISBN: *1-59462-286-8* **$34.45**
An interpretation of American democratic political theory. It examines political mechanics and society from the perspective of Scotsman James Bryce Politics Pages 572

Stories of the Pilgrims *by Margaret P. Pumphrey* ISBN: *1-59462-116-0* **$17.95**
This book explores pilgrims religious oppression in England as well as their escape to Holland and eventual crossing to America on the Mayflower, and their early days in New England... History Pages 268

QTY

The Fasting Cure by *Sinclair Upton*   ISBN: *1-59462-222-1* **$13.95**
In the Cosmopolitan Magazine for May, 1910, and in the Contemporary Review (London) for April, 1910, I published an article dealing with my experiences in fasting. I have written a great many magazine articles, but never one which attracted so much attention... New Age/Self Help/Health Pages 164

Hebrew Astrology by *Sepharial*   ISBN: *1-59462-308-2* **$13.45**
In these days of advanced thinking it is a matter of common observation that we have left many of the old landmarks behind and that we are now pressing forward to greater heights and to a wider horizon than that which represented the mind-content of our progenitors... Astrology Pages 144

Thought Vibration or The Law of Attraction in the Thought World   ISBN: *1-59462-127-6* **$12.95**
by William Walker Atkinson   *Psychology/Religion Pages 144*

Optimism by *Helen Keller*   ISBN: *1-59462-108-X* **$15.95**
Helen Keller was blind, deaf, and mute since 19 months old, yet famously learned how to overcome these handicaps, communicate with the world, and spread her lectures promoting optimism. An inspiring read for everyone... Biographies/Inspirational Pages 84

Sara Crewe by *Frances Burnett*   ISBN: *1-59462-360-0*   **$9.45**
In the first place, Miss Minchin lived in London. Her home was a large, dull, tall one, in a large, dull square, where all the houses were alike, and all the sparrows were alike, and where all the door-knockers made the same heavy sound... Childrens/Classic Pages 88

The Autobiography of Benjamin Franklin by *Benjamin Franklin*   ISBN: *1-59462-135-7* **$24.95**
The Autobiography of Benjamin Franklin has probably been more extensively read than any other American historical work, and no other book of its kind has had such ups and downs of fortune. Franklin lived for many years in England, where he was agent... Biographies/History Pages 332

Name	
Email	
Telephone	
Address	
City, State ZIP	

☐ **Credit Card**   ☐ **Check / Money Order**

Credit Card Number	
Expiration Date	
Signature	

Please Mail to: Book Jungle
PO Box 2226
Champaign, IL 61825
or Fax to: 630-214-0564

ORDERING INFORMATION

web: *www.bookjungle.com*
email: *sales@bookjungle.com*
fax: *630-214-0564*
mail: *Book Jungle PO Box 2226 Champaign, IL 61825*
or PayPal *to sales@bookjungle.com*

Please contact us for bulk discounts

DIRECT-ORDER TERMS

**20% Discount if You Order
Two or More Books**
Free Domestic Shipping!
Accepted: Master Card, Visa,
Discover, American Express

www.ingramcontent.com/pod-product-compliance
Lightning Source LLC
LaVergne TN
LVHW061226060426
835509LV00012B/1442